Anonymous

The Manual of the Confraternity of the Blessed Sacrament

Of the Body and Blood of Christ

Anonymous

The Manual of the Confraternity of the Blessed Sacrament
Of the Body and Blood of Christ

ISBN/EAN: 9783744657310

Printed in Europe, USA, Canada, Australia, Japan

Cover: Foto ©Lupo / pixelio.de

More available books at **www.hansebooks.com**

The Manual

OF THE CONFRATERNITY OF

THE BLESSED S·ACRAMENT

OF THE

Body and Blood of Christ.

FIFTH EDITION.

London:

PRINTED FOR THE CONFRATERNITY AND SOLD BY

JOSEPH MASTERS, 78, NEW BOND STREET,

MDCCCLXXIII.

Contents.

PART I.

PART II.

Contents.

PART I.

PART II.

Short Office for Spiritual C

of our
LESSED
BLOOD.
at the
EUCHA-

the Ca-
of re-
fasting.

be pre-
greater
ys, when
ebrated,

Ave verum Corpus.

Hail to Thee! true Body sprung
  From the Virgin Mary's womb!
The Same that on the Cross was hung,
  And bore for man the bitter doom!
Hear us, merciful and mild,
JESU! Mary's gracious Child.   Amen.

From Whose Side for sinners riven
  Water flowed and mingled Blood!
May'st Thou, dearest LORD! be given
  In death's hour to be my Food!
Hear us, merciful and mild,
JESU! Mary's gracious Child.   Amen.

The Manual.

PART I.

Objects, Rules, &c.,

OF

THE CONFRATERNITY.

Objects.

1. The Honour due to the Person of our LORD JESUS CHRIST in the BLESSED SACRAMENT of His BODY and BLOOD.
2. Mutual and special Intercession at the time of and in union with the EUCHARISTIC SACRIFICE.
3. To promote the observance of the Catholic and primitive practice of receiving the Holy Communion fasting.

Rules.

1. To Communicate, or at least to be present, on Sundays and the greater Festivals, and other Holy-days, when the HOLY EUCHARIST is Celebrated,

unless prevented by sickness or other urgent cause.

2. To promote, by all legitimate means, frequent and reverent Celebrations of the HOLY EUCHARIST, as the Chief Act of Divine Service.

3. To make such special Intercessions as shall be from time to time directed.

Recommendations.

1. To give careful attention to Preparation before, and Thanksgiving after, every Communion.

2. To Communicate at an early Celebration.

3. To make, at every Celebration, one or more of the following Acts—
   Of Faith.
   Of Adoration.
   Of Spiritual Communion.
   Of Thanksgiving.
   Of Reparation.
   Of Intercession.
   Of Prayer for the Visible Unity of Christendom.

4. To make Acts of Spiritual Communion, when deprived of the opportunity of receiving the HOLY EUCHARIST.

5. To make Offerings for the due and reverent Celebration of the HOLY EUCHARIST.

Laws.

1. Constitution.

The Confraternity of the Blessed Sacrament of the Body and Blood of Christ shall consist of Bishops, Priests, and Deacons; Members of Brotherhoods and Sisterhoods; and Communicants of both sexes.

2. Form of Government.

The Confraternity shall be governed by
- 1. A Superior-General, and
- 2. A Council.

3. Membership.

Subject to the conditions herein set forth, any one being a Communicant or under preparation for receiving Holy Communion, shall be eligible to become an Associate of this Confraternity.

Such person being desirous of becoming an Associate of the Confraternity of the Blessed Sacrament, shall signify his, or her, wish to the Superior-General, or to one of the Superiors of the various Wards, or to any Priest-Associate in the following form :—

I, ——, being a (Bishop, Priest, Deacon, Brother or Sister of a Religious Com-

munity, or Communicant of the English Church,) do request to be admitted an Associate of the Confraternity of the Blessed Sacrament of the Body and Blood of Christ, and do hereby concur in its Objects, Rules, Recommendations and Laws.

> *Name in full* ....
> *Address* ....
> *Date* ....

I, ——, Associate, do recommend the aforesaid ——, to be admitted and enrolled among the Associates of this Confraternity.

Candidates shall be admitted to Membership by the Superior-General, a Superior of a Ward, or any Priest-Associate, according to a form hereinafter set forth.

Associates are invited to make offerings, according to their ability, to the General Fund of the Confraternity, from time to time, and especially upon the day of their admission.

4. THE SUPERIOR-GENERAL.

The Superior-General shall be either a Bishop, or Priest, elected annually at the Annual Meeting of the Council, subject to the approval of the Conference of Associates.

It shall be his duty to govern the Confraternity according to its Objects and Laws, with the advice of the Council.

5. The Superiors of Wards.

The Superiors of Wards shall be such Priests-Associate as have established Wards, or Branches of this Confraternity, with the consent of the Superior-General.

6. The Council.

The Council shall consist of the Superior-General, and the Superiors of Wards, together with such Priests-Associate as shall be elected for the year ensuing at the Annual Meeting of the Council, subject to the approval of the Conference of Associates.

The Council shall meet at least annually, previous to the Annual Conference of Associates, and at such other times as the Superior-General may direct.

The Superior-General upon the requisition of not less than three members of the Council, shall convene a meeting within fourteen days of the date thereof.

7. The Treasurer and Secretary or Secretaries.

There shall be a Treasurer and Secretary or Secretaries for the Confraternity, elected annually by the Council.

It shall be the duty of the Secretary to keep the Registers of the Confraternity, to send Notices, and to make arrangements for circulating subjects for Intercession among the members, under the direction of the Superior-General.

8. WARDS.

It shall be competent for each Ward to frame its own Regulations, in conformity with the Objects, Rules, and Recommendations of the Confraternity, subject to the approval of the Superior-General.

9. THE ANNUAL CONFERENCE.

The Annual Conference, open to all Associates of the Confraternity, shall be held on the first Thursday after Trinity Sunday, or within eight days of that date, after a Celebration of the HOLY EUCHARIST. And all Priests-Associate shall, within the same period, if possible, celebrate the HOLY EUCHARIST for the objects and intentions of the Confraternity, either in their own Churches, or in some neighbouring parish.

10. INTERCESSORY PRAYER.

Any person, whether an Associate of the Confraternity or not, may send direct to the Superior-General, or to him through any Priest-Associate, a request for the prayers of the Confraternity; and if approved by the Superior-General, the intercession shall be included in the Monthly List for such time as may be by him appointed.

The Monthly Paper shall be sent to all Associates of the Confraternity, through the Superiors of Wards or the Priests-Associate ; but in the case of Associates in Religious Communities, through their own spiritual Superiors.

11. Altar Linen and Vestments.

It is intended, according to the means placed at the disposal of the Council, to provide Altar Linen and Vestments for such poor parishes as may need such assistance.

Associates are specially invited to make offerings of alms, materials, or work for this purpose.

12. Alteration of Laws.

These Objects, Rules, Recommendations, and Laws, can only be altered by the Council, subject to the confirmation of the Annual Conference.

Instructions to Priests-Associate.

1. It is earnestly requested that Priests-Associate, on admitting members, will be careful to see that the obligations incurred by membership are clearly understood.

2. They are also requested, on admitting *a Priest* into the Confraternity, to give notice of such admission, together with the *full address* of the new Priest-Associate, without delay, to the Secretary, in order that his name may be registered, and the subjects for intercessory prayer and other notices be duly forwarded to him.

3. On admitting *a lay member* the Priest-Associate is requested to be careful to keep the name and address of the new member, as he will be responsible for the Monthly Paper and other notices being sent to such member.

4. Priests-Associate are also particularly requested to send the names and addresses of all *lay* Associates admitted by them during the past year to the Secretary on or before the Feast of the Ascension.

5. It is hoped that the greatest care and regularity will be taken in transmitting the notices for intercessory Prayer.

6. Persons desirous of becoming members of the Confraternity and duly recom-

mended, but unable to appear personally for admission before a Priest-Associate, may be provisionally admitted on the assurance of their intention to seek formal admission as soon as may be practicable.

7. Offerings made to the general fund of the Confraternity or for special purposes should be transmitted to the Treasurer.

8. Superiors of Wards should see that minutes of their proceedings are duly kept, as well as a list of the names and addresses of the Associates belonging to their Ward, or admitted by them.

On the Use of the Intercessions.

THE following suggestions are offered as to the use of the Monthly Papers of Intercession:—

It is not supposed that every intercession can be offered in full and separately at every Communion.

It would be sufficient if the intention of offering them in union with the body of Associates be made at every Communion.

The several intercessions may be read over some time before the Communion, and then offered in intention at the time of Communion.

Or the paper may be read carefully on a certain day in the week, say the Sunday in each week, and, if necessary, gone through

again in the interval; and then the subjects be borne in heart, at least in intention, at Communion.

Or a portion of the Paper may be read
over on one day of the week, the remain-
ing portions on other days, and all be offered together in intention.

The whole body of Associates will still
be united in a common bond of intercessory prayer, and all will still be offering together the same desires with one intention.

Should it happen in any case that even
this limited use of the intercessions is diffi-
cult, it will be sufficient simply to com-
memorate the objects by inserting in any
intercessory prayer, the mention, together
with any others specially remembered, "of
those who are being prayed for in the
Confraternity of the Blessed Sacrament of
the Body and Blood of CHRIST."

The Manual.

PART II.

Form for Blessing the Medal.

℣. Our Help is in the Name of the LORD:
℟. *Who hath made heaven and earth.*
℣. The LORD be with you:
℟. *And with thy spirit.*

Let us pray.

Bless, ✠ O LORD, this Medal, and grant that *he* (or *she*) who shall wear it may ever believe, [*if a priest*, teach,] speak, and do according to the truth of Thy Blessed Body and Blood in the Sacrament of the Altar, as shall be pleasing to Thee and profitable to *his* (or *her*) soul, Who livest and reignest, One GOD, world without end. *Amen.*

Office of Admission.

The Candidate to be admitted kneeling; the Superior of the Ward [or Priest-Associate] standing, shall say :

IN ✠ the Name of the FATHER, and of the SON, and of the HOLY GHOST. Amen.

c

WE wait for Thy Loving-kindness, O
  GOD, in the midst of Thy Temple.
O GOD, according to Thy Name, so is Thy
praise unto the world's end: Thy Right
Hand is full of Righteousness.

Let us pray.

LORD, have mercy upon us.
  CHRIST, *have mercy upon us.*
  LORD, have mercy upon us.

OUR FATHER, Which art in Heaven, Hallowed be Thy Name. Thy kingdom
come. Thy will be done in earth, as it is
in Heaven. Give us this day our daily
bread. And forgive us our trespasses, As
we forgive them that trespass against us.
And lead us not into temptation; But deliver us from evil. Amen.

O LORD, save this Thy servant:
  ℟. *Who putteth* his *trust in Thee.*
  ℣. Send *him* help, O LORD, from the
      sanctuary:
  ℟. *And strengthen* him *out of Sion.*
  ℣. Remember all *his* offerings:
  ℟. *And accept* his *burnt sacrifice.*
  ℣. Grant *him his* heart's desire:
  ℟. *And fulfil all* his *mind.*
  ℣. Let *him* rejoice in Thy Salvation:
  ℟. *And triumph in the Name of the*
      LORD his GOD.
  ℣. O LORD, hear our prayer:
  ℟. *And let our cry come unto Thee.*

℣. The LORD be with you:
℟. *And with thy spirit.*

Let us pray.

O LORD, JESU CHRIST, Who declarest Thine exceeding great Love in the most holy Sacrament of the Altar, we beseech Thee mercifully to assist us in these our supplications and prayers, and vouchsafe to receive *this* Thy servant now present before Thee, who desires to offer Thee special honour and worship in this adorable Mystery. Bless and sanctify *him* according to the multitude of Thy mercies; increase in *him* love and reverence for Thy Sacred Presence; bring forth in *him* the fruit of good living, and grant *him* steadfast perseverance unto the end, that hereafter *he* may behold, adore, and rejoice in Thy unveiled Presence in Heaven, where with the FATHER and the HOLY GHOST, Thou livest and reignest, One GOD, world without end. *Amen.*

O GOD, Who in this wonderful Sacrament hast left us a Memorial of Thy Passion; Grant us, we beseech Thee, so to venerate the Sacred Mysteries of Thy BODY and BLOOD, that we may ever feel within ourselves the fruit of Thy Redemption, Who livest and reignest, with the FATHER, in the Unity of the HOLY SPIRIT, GOD, for ever and ever. *Amen.*

The Superior, addressing the Person to be admitted, shall say :

DOST thou desire to be an Associate of the Confraternity of the BLESSED SACRAMENT?

Answer. I do.

Then the Superior shall say :

N., I ADMIT thee to be an Associate of the Confraternity of the BLESSED SACRAMENT of the BODY and BLOOD of CHRIST, in the Name of the FATHER, and of the SON, and of the HOLY GHOST. Amen.

The Superior, giving to the new Associate the Medal, shall say :

RECEIVE this Token of thy Membership in the Confraternity of the BLESSED SACRAMENT of the BODY and BLOOD of CHRIST, and see that thou fulfil in thy life what thou dost profess with thy lips.

The Superior shall then say :

THE LORD, the Fountain of all grace and mercy, ever in His Blessed Sacrament strengthen and renew you, guide and preserve you amid the storms of this world, and bring you into the haven of everlasting salvation. Amen.

After which may be said : '

PSALM CXI. *Confitebor Tibi.*

I WILL give thanks unto the LORD with my whole heart : secretly among the faithful, and in the congregation.

The works of the LORD are great : sought out of all them that have pleasure therein.

His work is worthy to be praised, and had in honour : and His righteousness endureth for ever.

The merciful and gracious LORD hath so done His marvellous works : that they ought to be had in remembrance.

He hath given meat unto them that fear Him : He shall ever be mindful of His covenant.

He hath showed His people the power of His works : that He may give them the heritage of the heathen.

The works of His Hands are verity and judgment : all His commandments are true.

They stand fast for ever and ever : and are done in truth and equity.

He sent redemption unto His people; He hath commanded His covenant for ever : holy and reverend is His Name.

The fear of the LORD is the beginning of wisdom : a good understanding have all they that do thereafter: the praise of it endureth for ever.

Glory be to the FATHER, and to the SON : and to the HOLY GHOST;

As it was in the beginning, is now, and ever shall be : world without end. Amen.

THE LORD be with you : ..

℣. Let us bless the LORD :
℟. *Thanks be to* GOD.

The Blessing.

THE Grace of our LORD JESUS CHRIST, and the Love of GOD, and the Fellowship of the HOLY GHOST, be with us all evermore.
℟. *Amen.*

Office for Ward Meetings.

IN ✠ the Name of the FATHER, and of the SON, and of the HOLY GHOST. Amen.

OUR FATHER, Which art in Heaven, Hallowed be Thy Name. Thy kingdom come. Thy will be done in earth, as it is in Heaven. Give us this day our daily bread. And forgive us our trespasses, As we forgive them that trespass against us. And lead us not into temptation; But deliver us from evil. Amen.

O GOD, make speed to save us :
℟. O LORD, *make haste to help us.*

℣. Glory be to the FATHER, and to the SON : and to the HOLY GHOST ;
℟. *As it was in the beginning, is now, and ever shall be, world without end. Amen.*

Or from Septuagesima to Easter.

Praise be to Thee, O LORD, King of eternal glory.

One or more of the Psalms following may then be used.

Antiphon. I will go unto the Altar of GOD.

PSALM XXVI. *Judica me, Domine.*

BE Thou my Judge, O LORD, for I have walked innocently : my trust hath been also in the LORD, therefore shall I not fall.

Examine me, O LORD, and prove me : try out my reins and my heart.

For Thy loving-kindness is ever before mine eyes : and I will walk in Thy truth.

I have not dwelt with vain persons : neither will I have fellowship with the deceitful.

I have hated the congregation of the wicked : and will not sit among the ungodly.

I will wash my hands in innocency, O LORD : and so will I go to Thine Altar;

That I may show the voice of thanks-. giving : and tell of all Thy wondrous works.

LORD, I have loved the habitation of Thy house : and the place where Thine honour dwelleth.

O shut not up my soul with the sinners : nor my life with the blood-thirsty ;

In whose hands is wickedness : and their

But as for me, I will walk innocently :
O deliver me and be merciful unto me.

My foot standeth right : I will praise
the LORD in the congregations.

Glory be to the FATHER, and to the SON :
and to the HOLY GHOST;

As it was in the beginning, is now, and
ever shall be : world without end. Amen.

PSALM XLIII. *Judica me, Deus.*

GIVE sentence with me, O GOD, and
defend my cause against the ungodly
people : O deliver me from the deceitful
and wicked man.

For Thou art the GOD of my strength; why
hast Thou put me from Thee : and why go I
so heavily, while the enemy oppresseth me?

O send out Thy light and Thy truth,
that they may lead me : and bring me unto Thy holy hill, and to Thy dwelling.

And that I may go unto the Altar of
GOD, even unto the GOD of my joy and
gladness : and upon the harp will I give
thanks unto Thee, O GOD, my GOD.

Why art thou so heavy, O my soul :
and why art thou so disquieted within me?

O put thy trust in GOD : for I will yet
give Him thanks, which is the help of my
countenance, and my GOD.

Glory be to the FATHER, and to the
SON : and to the HOLY GHOST;

As it was in the beginning, is now, and

PSALM CXVI. 10. *Credidi.*

I BELIEVED, and therefore will I speak; but I was sore troubled : I said in my haste, All men are liars.

What reward shall I give unto the LORD for all the benefits that He hath done unto me ?

I will receive the Cup of Salvation : and call upon the Name of the LORD.

I will pay my vows now in the presence of all His people : right dear in the sight of the LORD is the death of His saints.

Behold, O LORD, how that I am Thy servant : I am Thy servant, and the son of Thine handmaid; Thou hast broken my bonds in sunder.

I will offer to Thee the Sacrifice of thanksgiving : and will call upon the Name of the LORD.

I will pay my vows unto the LORD, in the sight of all His people : in the courts of the LORD's house, even in the midst of thee, O Jerusalem. Praise the LORD.

Glory be to the FATHER, and to the SON : and to the HOLY GHOST;

As it was in the beginning, is now, and ever shall be : world without end. Amen.

Antiphon. I will go unto the Altar of GOD, even unto the GOD of my joy and

SHORT LESSON. 1 *Cor*. x. 16, 17.

THE Cup of Blessing which we bless, is it not the Communion of the Blood of CHRIST? The Bread which we break, is it not the Communion of the Body of CHRIST?

For we being many are one Bread, and one Body; for we are all partakers of that one Bread.

R⁒. *Thanks be to* GOD.

A CERTAIN Man made a great supper, and sent His servants at supper time to say to them that were bidden, Come, for all things are now ready.

R⁒. *A certain Man made a great supper,*
and sent His servants at supper time
to say to them that were bidden,
Come, for all things are now ready.

℣. Come, eat of My Bread, and drink of the Wine which I have mingled.
R⁒. *For all things are now ready.*
℣. Glory be to the FATHER, and to the SON, and to the HOLY GHOST.
R⁒. *For all things are now ready.*

HYMN. *Pange lingua gloriosi.*

Now, my tongue, the mystery telling
  Of the glorious Body sing,
And the Blood, all price excelling,
  Which the Gentiles' LORD and King,
In a Virgin's womb once dwelling,

Given for us, and condescending
To be born for us below,
He with men in converse blending
Dwelt the seed of truth to sow,
Till He closed with wondrous ending
His most patient life of woe.

That last night at Supper lying,
'Mid the twelve, His chosen band,
JESUS, with the law complying,
Keeps the feast its rites demand;
Then more precious Food supplying,
Gives Himself with His Own Hand.

Word-made-Flesh true bread He maketh
By His Word His Flesh to be;
Wine, His Blood; which whoso taketh
Must from carnal thoughts be free;
Faith alone, though sight forsaketh,
Shows true hearts the Mystery.

Therefore we, before Him bending,
This great Sacrament revere;
Types and shadows have their ending,
For the newer Rite is here;
Faith, our outward sense befriending,
Makes our inward vision clear.

Glory let us give, and blessing,
To the FATHER and the SON,
Honour, might, and praise addressing,
While eternal ages run:
Ever too, His love confessing,
Who from Both with Both is One. Amen.

℣. Thou gavest them Bread from Heaven. [Alleluia.]

℟. *Containing in Itself all sweetness.* [*Alleluia.*]

Antiphon. O Sacred Banquet.

MAGNIFICAT. *S. Luke* i.

MY soul doth magnify the LORD : and my spirit hath rejoiced in GOD my SAVIOUR.

For He hath regarded : the lowliness of His handmaiden.

For behold, from henceforth : all generations shall call me blessed.

For He that is mighty hath magnified me : and holy is His Name.

And His mercy is on them that fear Him : throughout all generations.

He hath showed strength with His arm : He hath scattered the proud in the imagination of their hearts.

He hath put down the mighty from their seat : and hath exalted the humble and meek.

He hath filled the hungry with good things : and the rich He hath sent empty away.

He remembering His mercy hath holpen His servant Israel : as He promised to our forefathers, Abraham and his seed for ever.

Glory be to the FATHER, and to the SON : and to the HOLY GHOST;

As it was in the beginning, is now, and ever shall be : world without end. Amen.

Antiphon. O Sacred Banquet in which CHRIST is received, the memory of His Passion renewed, the mind filled with Grace, and a Pledge of future Glory given unto us. [Alleluia.]

Note : here may follow an Instruction by the Priest, with one of the Litanies ; or the Office may thus be concluded.

LORD, have mercy upon us.
   CHRIST, *have mercy upon us.*
Lord, have mercy upon us.

OUR FATHER, Which art in Heaven, Hallowed be Thy Name. Thy kingdom come. Thy will be done in earth, as it is in Heaven. Give us this day our daily bread. And forgive us our trespasses, As we forgive them that trespass against us. And lead us not into temptation ; But deliver us from evil. Amen.

I SAID, LORD, have mercy upon me :
   R̰. *Heal my soul, for I have sinned against Thee.*

   ℣. He healeth those that are broken in heart :

R̰. *And giveth Medicine to heal their sickness.*

V̰. He maketh peace in thy borders :

R̰. *And filleth thee with the flour of wheat.*

V̰. O taste and see how gracious the LORD is :

R̰. *For Thou, O LORD, hast of Thy goodness prepared for the poor.*

V̰. The Memorial of Thine abundant kindness shall be showed :

R̰. *And men shall sing of Thy righteousness.*

V̰. The eyes of all wait upon Thee, O LORD :

R̰. *And Thou givest them their Meat in due season.*

V̰. Thou openest Thine Hand :

R̰. *And fillest all things living with plenteousness.*

V̰. O LORD, hear our prayer :

R̰. *And let our cry come unto Thee.*

V̰. The LORD be with you :

R̰. *And with thy spirit.*

Let us pray.

O GOD, Who in this Wonderful Sacrament hast left us a Memorial of Thy Passion ; Grant us, we beseech Thee, so to venerate the Sacred Mysteries of Thy BODY and BLOOD, that we may ever feel within ourselves the fruit of Thy redemption, Who livest and reignest with the FATHER in the Unity of the HOLY SPIRIT, GOD, for ever and ever. *Amen.*

Or this :

O GOD, Who dost wonderfully refresh Thy Church by Thy precious BODY and BLOOD : pour out upon it Thy quickening SPIRIT, that, living upon Thee on earth, through partaking of the Heavenly Mysteries, we may attain to live with Thee in Heaven, Who livest and reignest with the FATHER and the HOLY GHOST, One GOD, world without end. *Amen.*

Here the Prayer for the Confraternity, page 39, or other Collects or Prayers may be added.

THE LORD be with you :
R̷. *And with thy spirit.*

℣. Let us bless the LORD :
R̷. *Thanks be to* GOD.

MAY the souls of the Faithful Departed, through the Mercy of GOD, rest in peace.
R̷. *Amen.*

Acts of Devotion and Prayers.

The following Acts of Devotion and Prayers are not obligatory upon the Associates, nor intended to supersede other similar Acts and Prayers, which may for any reason be preferred.

Acts of Faith.

O MY beloved LORD and SAVIOUR, JESU CHRIST, I firmly believe, because Thou hast said, "THIS IS MY BODY; THIS IS MY BLOOD," that in this blessed Sacrament Thou art truly present, Thy Divinity and Thy Humanity, with all the treasures of Thy merits and Thy Grace : that Thou art Thyself mystically offered for us in this Holy Oblation ; and dost through Thy Own Presence communicate the virtues of Thy most precious Death and Passion to all Thy Faithful, living and departed.

I beseech Thee, that Thy Holy Spirit may increase and quicken my faith; kindle all the desires of my soul; inflame me with raptures of love, of thankfulness, and joy; and give me grace to approach Thee with the reverence and humility due to Thy Majesty, and to receive Thee in most intimate Communion with a cleansed conscience and a pure heart. Amen.

Or this:

O GOD, Whose Blessed Son Jesus Christ was called of Thee a High Priest for ever, after the order of Melchizedek, and Who, on the same night in which He was betrayed, said, taking bread and wine into His Sacred Hands, "This is My Body, This is My Blood; Do this in remembrance of Me;" thus "teaching us the Oblation of the New Covenant, which the Church receiving from the Apostles offers to Thee throughout the whole world," have mercy upon us miserable sinners. Send us, as Thou promisedst, the "Corn, and Wine, and Oil" of gladness, that we may be "satisfied therewith, and be no more a reproach among the heathen."

Grant, O Lord, that we being jealous for the truth of Thy Word, may continually offer to Thee this our "Pure Offering," and may evermore glorify Thee in Thy Holy Church, through the Same Jesus Christ, our Lord and High Priest, Who liveth and reigneth with Thee and the Holy Ghost, ever One God, world without end. Amen.

Act of Adoration.

I ADORE Thee, O Lord my God, Whom I now behold veiled beneath these

earthly forms. Prostrate I adore Thy
Majesty, and because, sinful and unworthy that I am, I cannot honour Thee as I
ought, I unite myself with Thy Saints and
Angels in their more perfect adoration.

Hail, most HOLY BODY of CHRIST! Hail,
Living Bread, that comest down from hea-
ven to give life to the world! Hail, most
HOLY BLOOD of JESUS, shed for sinners!
Above all things the sum and fulness of
delight! Hail, saving Victim, offered for
me and for all mankind! CHRIST, Eternal
King! Man, crucified for man!

Behold, I praise, I bless, I glorify Thee.
I would that all might glorify Thee in this
Mystery of Thy love. And grant to me
that, dying to the world and living here a
life hidden in Thee, I may hereafter see
Thy Face unveiled, to love and adore and
rejoice in Thee, through all eternity. Amen.

Act of Spiritual Communion.

O MOST Loving JESU! most Blessed
SAVIOUR! Spouse of holy souls!
come to me, I beseech Thee, and unite Thyself with me, pervading all my substance,
and flow even through all my senses and
faculties, that I may be dissolved in love.

[Though I cannot now receive Thee sacramentally, yet I believe that Thou art
able, even when received by faith and de-

sire only, perfectly to heal, enrich, and
sanctify me ; and, I beseech Thee, grant
me this grace, while hindered from more
perfect union with Thee.][1]

Come, Thou Life of my soul, rule me
and every movement of my being with
an absolute dominion, that I being in-
corporated into Thee, and Thou in me,
every hateful desire and affection may be
quenched in me, and every virtue matured
in me, after Thy likeness.

Possess me wholly ; let the consuming
fire of Thy love absorb me, and Thy Presence abide so intimately one with me,
that it is no longer I that live, but Thou
Who livest in me. Amen.

Act of Thanksgiving.

I OFFER thanks to Thee, O LORD, Holy
FATHER, Almighty, Everlasting GOD,
because, not for any merit of mine, but of
the condescension of Thy mercy only,
Thou hast given Thyself to me a sinner.
I am filled with a thrilling sense of thankfulness, and love. My soul exults, and
adores, and praises Thee, O LORD, my
GOD, my JESU, my Redeemer ; for Thou
hast spoken and said, *Whoso eateth My*

[1] This is intended to be said only by those
who are hindered from Sacramental Communion.

Flesh, and drinketh My Blood, dwelleth in Me, and I in him. O Joy beyond all joys! to possess Thee enshrined within my bosom; to embrace Thee with all the fervour of my heart; to be *flesh of Thy Flesh, and bone of Thy Bone;* to be of one Body and one Spirit with Thee, the Eternal, the Incomprehensible, the All-Holy GOD.

Wherefore in this blissful confidence of my perfect union with Thee, O my GOD, I devote myself wholly to Thee, beseeching Thee to shed forth within me the fulness of Thy Grace, that all my faculties of soul and body, every sense, thought, affection, desire, may be concentrated and absorbed in the one end of loving and serving Thee, ever more and more. Amen.

Act of Reparation.

O LORD, my GOD and SAVIOUR, Who, as Thou didst endure for our salvation the outrages of those who crucified Thee, so now deignest to bear with those who approach and touch Thee, "not discerning" Thee, and endurest all irreverences, rather than withhold Thy Sacred Presence from our Altars; I bewail these indignities, and most earnestly desire to prevent, to the utmost of my power, whatever thus still grieves Thee.

I beseech Thee, accept this sorrow and this desire, as the only offering I can make in reparation of so great dishonour. O LORD, increase our faith, and preserve us from the least profanation of this adorable Mystery, and kindle in me and in the hearts of all Thy people, especially of all who celebrate or assist in Its ministration, such reverence and devotion, that Thy most holy Name may more and more be honoured and glorified in this Sacrament of love. Amen.

Acts of Intercession.

O ALMIGHTY FATHER, look favourably upon us, we beseech Thee, and accept this most Holy Sacrifice of praise and propitiation, Which we offer to Thee in union with the Oblation Which our LORD JESUS CHRIST offers unceasingly in the Heavens ; and by His meritorious sufferings, and by all His Love, have mercy upon all for whom He died,—that they who know Thee not, may be brought to the knowledge and love of the truth ; that Thy whole Church may be replenished with the fruits of Thy holiness ; that all sinners may be converted to Thee ; that all Thy faithful, struggling through trial, in weakness or suffering, spiritual or bodily, may be strengthened and refreshed ;

that all departed this life with the seal of faith, especially those who have been united with us in this Confraternity, may rest in peace, and that we with them, purified from all earthly stains, may attain to the Fulness of everlasting Joy.　Amen.

Or this :

ALMIGHTY God, we beseech Thee to hear our prayers for such as sin against Thee, or neglect to serve Thee [especially . . . .], that Thou wouldest vouchsafe to bestow upon them true repentance and earnest longing for Thy service; through Jesus Christ our Lord.　Amen.

Prayers for the Visible Unity of Christendom.

O GOD, Who art One God, though in Three Persons, Blessed for evermore, Who hast predestined us to glorify Thee in one Body in Thy Only-begotten Son, we earnestly pray Thee for the restoration of visible unity of worship and communion between the divided members of the Catholic Church, in the East and in the West; and that all who confess Thy holy Name, and are called Christians, may be re-united, as at the beginning, " in the Apostles' doctrine, and the fellowship, and in the breaking of the Bread, and in the Prayers."

Remove, we beseech Thee, from us, and from all others, whatever may hinder or delay this blessed re-union, all suspicions, prejudices, hard thoughts and judgments ; and endue us with such ardent love toward Thee, and toward each other, that we may be one in heart, even as Thou, LORD, art One with the FATHER, to Whom in the Unity of the HOLY GHOST, be all praise and glory and thanksgiving for ever. Amen.

Or this :

O LORD JESU CHRIST, Who saidst unto Thine Apostles, Peace I leave with you, My peace I give unto you ; regard not my sins, but the faith of Thy Church, and grant her that peace and unity which is agreeable to Thy will, Who livest and reignest, GOD, for ever and ever. Amen.

Prayer for the Confraternity.

O ALMIGHTY and Eternal GOD, we humbly pray Thee to vouchsafe Thy blessing to this Confraternity, that all the Associates, being inspired with lively faith and love, may earnestly strive to promote the Honour due to Thy dear SON, JESUS CHRIST, in the BLESSED SACRAMENT of His BODY and BLOOD. Enable us, both Priests and people, who are joined together in this special bond, to help one another with mutual intercessions, and give us grace to fulfil in our lives what we have professed with our lips. Deliver us, O GOD, from all false doctrine and slackness of living; and grant that persevering unto the end in the faith, practice and communion of Thy Holy Church, we may all at length attain by a holy and peaceful death to the joy and light of everlasting life; through the Same JESUS CHRIST our LORD. Amen.

Prayers suggested for Daily Use.

O ALMIGHTY GOD, look, we beseech Thee, on the Face of Thy Beloved SON, and for the sake of His merits, mercifully hear the prayers which throughout our Confraternity we continually offer to Thee [especially . . . . .], and grant us unity, a true faith, and a life agreeable to Thy will; through JESUS CHRIST our LORD. Amen.

Another:

BLESSED, praised, and hallowed be JESUS CHRIST on His Throne of glory, and in the Most Holy Sacrament of the Altar. Amen.

Litany of our Lord Present in the Holy Eucharist.

LORD, have mercy upon us.
CHRIST, *have mercy upon us.*
LORD, have mercy upon us.

O CHRIST, hear us.
O CHRIST, *graciously hear us.*

GOD the FATHER, Creator of the world;
Have mercy upon us.

GOD the SON, Redeemer of mankind;
Have mercy upon us.

GOD the HOLY GHOST, Perfecter of the elect;
Have mercy upon us.

HOLY TRINITY, Three Persons, One GOD;
Have mercy upon us.

JESU, GOD and Man, in Two Natures and One Divine Person;
Have mercy upon us.

JESU, our Wonderful GOD, Who vouchsafest to be Present upon the Altar when

the Priest pronounces the words of Consecration ;
Have mercy upon us.

JESU, our Heavenly Physician, Who vouchsafest to descend from Thy Palace of immortal bliss to our houses of clay, to visit us on beds of sickness, and to give Thyself to comfort our sorrows ;
Have mercy upon us.

JESU, our Incomprehensible GOD, Who, though the Heaven of Heavens cannot contain Thee, art pleased to dwell among men ;
Have mercy upon us.

JESU, our Sovereign King, Who, though Thy Throne is attended by glorified Spirits, yet declinest not the service of men ;
Have mercy upon us.

JESU, our Glorious GOD, Who sittest at the Right Hand of Thy Eternal FATHER, adored by innumerable Angels, and encompassed with the splendours of inaccessible Light ;
Have mercy upon us.

JESU, our Gracious GOD, Who, condescending to the weakness of our nature, coverest Thy Glory under the familiar Forms of Bread and Wine, and so givest Thyself to miserable sinners ;
Have mercy upon us.

JESU, our Merciful GOD, Who, concealing the brightness of Thy majesty under these low and humble Veils, invitest us to approach unto Thee, to lay open our miseries before Thy Eyes, and to deliver our petitions into Thy hands;
Have mercy upon us.

JESU, our Pitiful GOD, Who, to communicate Thy Divine Nature to sinners, humblest Thyself to descend into our hearts, and, by an inconceivable Union, to become One with us;
Have mercy upon us.

JESU, the Bread of Life, Which camest down from Heaven, of Which whosoever eats shall live for ever;
Have mercy upon us.

JESU, the Heavenly Manna, Whose sweetness nourisheth Thy elect in the desert of this world;
Have mercy upon us.

JESU, the Food of Angels, Whose sweetness filleth our hearts with Celestial joys;
Have mercy upon us.

JESU, the Lamb without spot, Who, once sacrificed, art continually offered, yet art alive for evermore; Who art continually consumed, yet still remainest Perfect;
Have mercy upon us.

JESU, the Good Shepherd, Who layest down Thy Life for Thy Sheep, and feedest them with Thine Own Body;
Have mercy upon us.

JESU, Who, in this August and Venerable Mystery, art Thyself both Priest and Victim;
Have mercy upon us.

JESU, Who in the Sacred Memorial of Thy Death, hast consummated all Thy wonders into one stupendous Miracle;
Have mercy upon us.

JESU, Who, in this Adorable Mystery, hast contracted all Thy Blessings into one inestimable Bounty;
Have mercy upon us.

JESU, Who, by this blessed Fruit of the Tree of Life, restorest us again to Immortality;
Have mercy upon us.

JESU, Who by becoming Thyself our Daily Food in this life, preparest us to feed on Thee for ever in the next;
Have mercy upon us.

JESU, Who, in this Divine Banquet, givest us possession of Thy Grace here, and a certain Pledge of our Glory hereafter;
Have mercy upon us.

JESU, Who art the Way, the Truth, and

the Life, and through Whom alone we approach the FATHER ;
Have mercy upon us.

SPARE us, Good LORD ;
And pardon our sins.

Spare us, Good LORD ;
And hear our prayers.

FROM presuming to measure the depth of Thy Almightiness by the short line of human reason ;
Good LORD, *deliver us.*

From presuming to interpret the unsearchable Secrets of Thy Will by the fallible rule of man's judgment ;
Good LORD, *deliver us.*

From all distraction and irreverence when present at this Awful Sacrifice ;
Good LORD, *deliver us.*

From neglecting to approach Thy Holy Table, and from coming to It unprepared ;
Good LORD, *deliver us.*

From an unworthy and fruitless reception of this Adorable Mystery ;
Good LORD, *deliver us.*

From all hardness of heart, and ingratitude for so unspeakable a Blessing ;
Good LORD, *deliver us.*

BY Thine irresistible Power, which changeth the course of Nature as Thou willest;
Good LORD, *deliver us.*

By Thine Unsearchable Wisdom, which disposeth all things in perfect order ;
Good LORD, *deliver us.*

By Thine Infinite Goodness, which freely bestoweth Thyself in this incomprehensible Mystery ;
Good LORD, *deliver us.*

By Thy most Sacred Body broken for us, and really given to us in the Holy Communion ;
Good LORD, *deliver us.*

By Thy most Precious Blood poured out for us on the Cross, and really given unto us in the Cup of Blessing ;
Good LORD, *deliver us.*

WE sinners most humbly beseech Thee;
To hear us, O LORD JESU CHRIST.

And that it may please Thee to grant,

THAT we may always believe nothing more reasonable than to submit our reason unto Thee ;
We beseech Thee to hear us, Good LORD.

That by this Sacred Oblation we may acknowledge Thine infinite Perfections in

Thyself and Thy supreme Dominion over all things ;
We beseech Thee to hear us, Good LORD.

That by this adorable Sacrifice we may acknowledge our perpetual dependence upon Thee, and our absolute subjection to Thy Will ;
We beseech Thee to hear us, Good LORD.

That we may ever magnify Thy Goodness, Who, having no need of us, hast set forth such endearing motives to make us love Thee ;
We beseech Thee to hear us, Good LORD.

That we may thankfully comply with Thy gracious Desire of being united to us, by a fervent desire of being made one with Thee ;
We beseech Thee to hear us, Good LORD.

That before we approach the Banquet of Divine Love, we may endeavour to be reconciled to Thee, and to be in perfect charity with all the world ;
We beseech Thee to hear us, Good LORD.

That, at the moment of receiving Thy Sacred Body and Thy Precious Blood, our souls may dissolve in reverence and love, to attend on and entertain so Glorious a Guest ;
We beseech Thee to hear us, Good LORD.

That returning from the Holy Eucharist, we may collect all our thoughts to praise and bless Thee, and strive to live after Thy Commandments ;
We beseech Thee to hear us, Good LORD.

That, by this Heavenly Medicine, our heart may be healed of all infirmities, and our will strengthened against all relapses ;
We beseech Thee to hear us, Good LORD.

That, as by faith we adore Thee Present beneath the Sacred Veils, we may hereafter behold Thee Face to face, and evermore be glad with the joy of Thy Countenance ;
We beseech Thee to hear us, Good LORD.

O LAMB of GOD, That takest away the sins of the world ;
Have mercy upon us.

O LAMB of GOD, That takest away the sins of the world ;
Have mercy upon us.

O LAMB of GOD, That takest away the sins of the world ;
Grant us Thy peace.

O CHRIST, hear us.
O CHRIST, *graciously hear us.*

Here the Litany may end, or proceed as follows :

LORD, have mercy upon us.
  CHRIST, *have mercy upon us.*
  LORD, have mercy upon us.

OUR FATHER, Which art in Heaven, Hallowed be Thy Name. Thy kingdom come. Thy will be done in earth, as it is in Heaven. Give us this day our daily bread. And forgive us our trespasses, As we forgive them that trespass against us. And lead us not into temptation; But deliver us from evil. Amen.

Antiphon. O Sacred Banquet, in which CHRIST is received, the memory of His Passion renewed, the mind filled with Grace, and a Pledge of Future Glory given unto us. [Alleluia.]
  ℣. Thou gavest them Bread from Heaven. [Alleluia.]
  ℟. *Containing in Itself all sweetness.* [*Alleluia.*]

Let us pray.
O GOD, Who in this Wonderful Sacrament hast left us a Memorial of Thy Passion; Grant us, we beseech Thee, so to venerate the sacred mysteries of Thy BODY and BLOOD, that we may ever feel within ourselves the fruit of Thy Redemption, Who livest and reignest with the FATHER in the Unity of the HOLY SPIRIT, GOD, for ever and ever. *Amen.*

Rhythm.   Anima Christi.

To be said together.

SOUL of CHRIST, sanctify me :
    Body of CHRIST, save me :
Blood of CHRIST, inebriate me :
Water from the Side of CHRIST, wash me :
Passion of CHRIST, strengthen me :
O Good JESU, hear me :
Within Thy Wounds hide me :
Suffer me not to be separated from Thee :
From the malicious enemy defend me :
In the hour of my death call me,
And bid me come unto Thee ;
That with Thy Saints I may praise Thee
For all eternity.   Amen.

O ALMIGHTY GOD, look, we beseech
    Thee, on the Face of Thy Beloved
SON, and, for the sake of His merits,
mercifully hear the prayers which throughout our Confraternity we continually offer
to Thee [especially . . . .] ; and grant us
unity, a true faith, and a life agreeable
to Thy Will; through the same JESUS
CHRIST our LORD.   *Amen.*

The Blessing.

MAY the LORD grant us His Peace, and
    Life Eternal.
   ℟. *Amen.*

Litany of the Blessed Sacrament.

IN METRE FOR SINGING.

LORD, have mercy upon us.
Lord, have mercy upon us.
CHRIST, have mercy upon us.
Christ, have mercy upon us.
LORD, have mercy upon us.
Lord, have mercy upon us.

O CHRIST, hear us.
Graciously hear us, O CHRIST.

GOD the FATHER, GOD the SON,
HOLY GHOST, the Comforter,
Ever-Blessed THREE in ONE,
Spare us, HOLY TRINITY.

BREAD of Life, from Heaven come down,
Hidden GOD and SAVIOUR,
Sacrifice for ever One,
Save us, O Sweet JESU.

Bread of Fatness, Royal Food,
Wine, whose fruit are Virgins,
Holiest of all Sacrifice,
Save us, O Sweet JESU.

Spotless LAMB of GOD Most High,
On the heavenly Altar seen,
Priest and Victim, both in One,
Save us, O Sweet JESU.

Hallowed Corn of GOD's elect,
Cup of Blessing filled for us,
Hidden Manna, Angels' Food,
 Save us, O Sweet JESU.

WORD made Flesh, 'neath earthly veils,
Atonement of the guilty soul,
Marvel of exceeding Love,
 Save us, O Sweet JESU.

Pledge of Thine Eternal Gifts,
Memorial of Thy Passion,
Heavenly Antidote for death,
 Save us, O Sweet JESU.

Bread made Flesh by Thine Own Word,
Gift surpassing all our hopes,
Food, and Sharer of the Feast,
 Save us, O Sweet JESU.

Medicine of Eternal Life,
August and Holy Mystery,
Purest Offering, Paschal Lamb,
 Save us, O Sweet JESU.

Fountain-head of Life and Love,
Pledge of future Glory,
Nourishment of holy souls,
 Save us, O Sweet JESU.

FROM all frail and worldly thoughts,
 From the unworthy reception
Of Thy Body and Thy Blood,
 Deliver us, O JESU.

From the lust of sinful flesh,
From the lust of wandering eyes,
From the pride of worldly life,
  Deliver us, O JESU.

By the Desire wherewith, ere death,
Thou desiredst with the Twelve
Thy last Paschal Feast to eat,
  Deliver us, O JESU.

By that deep Humility
Wherewith Thou didst wash their feet,
Giving the new law of love,
  Deliver us, O JESU.

By that burning Love of Thine,
Moving Thee to institute
This most Holy Sacrament,
  Deliver us, O JESU.

By the Sacred Testament
Of Thine Own most Precious Blood
To our Altars left by Thee,
  Deliver us, O JESU.

By Thy Body's Five blest Wounds,
Thy torn Hands and pierced Feet,
And Thy Heart Which bled with love,
  Deliver us, O JESU.

By the Bleeding Crown of thorns,
Which the world's lost empire won,
When Thy Head was bowed in death,
  Deliver us, O JESU.

THAT it may please Thee to increase
    Faith in us, and reverence
Towards this Blessed Sacrament,
    Hear us, Holy JESU.

That it may please Thee grace to give,
That with souls absolved and free
We may oft approach the Feast,
    Hear us, Holy JESU.

That it may please Thee to preserve
All Thy flock from heresy.
And from blindness of the heart,
    Hear us, Holy JESU.

That it may please Thee to impart
All the rich and heavenly Fruits
Of this Holy Sacrament,
    Hear us, Holy JESU.

That it may please Thee life to give,
In the strength of that blest Meat
Safe to tread the path of death,
    Hear us, Holy JESU.

O LAMB of GOD, That takest away the
    sins of the world ;
    Spare us, O LORD.

    O LAMB of GOD, That takest away the
sins of the world ;
    Graciously hear us, O LORD.

    O LAMB of GOD, That takest away the
sins of the world ;
    Have mercy upon us.

O CHRIST, hear us.
Graciously hear us, O CHRIST.

Here the Litany may end, or proceed as follows :

LORD, have mercy upon us.
CHRIST, *have mercy upon us.*
LORD, have mercy upon us.

OUR FATHER, Which art in Heaven, Hallowed be Thy Name. Thy kingdom come. Thy will be done in earth, as it is in Heaven. Give us this day our daily bread. And forgive us our trespasses, As we forgive them that trespass against us. And lead us not into temptation ; But deliver us from evil. Amen.

℣. Thou gavest them Bread from Heaven. [Alleluia.]
℟. *Containing in Itself all sweetness.* [*Alleluia.*]

Let us pray.

O GOD, Who, in this Wonderful Sacrament, hast left us a Memorial of Thy Passion ; Grant us, we beseech Thee, so to venerate the Sacred Mysteries of Thy BODY and BLOOD, that we may ever feel within ourselves the fruit of Thy Redemption, Who livest and reignest with the FATHER, in the Unity of the HOLY SPIRIT, GOD. for ever and ever. *Amen.*

Or this:

O GOD, Who dost wonderfully refresh Thy Church by Thy Precious Body and Blood; pour out upon it Thy Quickening SPIRIT, that, living upon Thee on earth, through partaking of the Heavenly Mysteries, we may attain to live with Thee in Heaven, Who livest and reignest with the FATHER and the HOLY GHOST, One GOD, world without end. *Amen.*

O ALMIGHTY GOD, look, we beseech Thee, on the Face of Thy Beloved SON, and, for the sake of His Merits, mercifully hear the prayers which throughout our Confraternity we continually offer to Thee [especially . . . . . .]; and grant us unity, a true faith, and a life agreeable to Thy Will; through the same JESUS CHRIST our LORD. *Amen.*

THE LORD be with you:
℞. *And with thy spirit.*

℣. Let us bless the LORD:
℞. *Thanks be to GOD.*

The Blessing.

MAY the Almighty and Merciful LORD, FATHER, SON, and HOLY GHOST, bless and preserve us.
℞. *Amen.*

Litany of Reparation.

LORD, have mercy upon us.
  CHRIST, *have mercy upon us.*
  LORD, have mercy upon us.

CHRIST, hear us.
  CHRIST, *graciously hear us.*

O GOD the FATHER of Mercies;
  Have mercy upon us.

O GOD the SON, Mediator between GOD and man;
  Have mercy upon us.

O GOD the HOLY GHOST, the Enlightener of hearts;
  Have mercy upon us.

O Holy and Undivided TRINITY;
  Have mercy upon us.

O SACRED Victim, offered in satisfaction for the sins of the world;
  Have mercy upon us.

O Sacred Victim, consumed on the Altar by us and for us;
  Have mercy upon us.

O Sacred Victim, despised and neglected by careless Christians;
  Have mercy upon us.

O Sacred Victim, outraged by the blasphemies of sinful men;
Have mercy upon us.

O Sacred Victim, abandoned by Thine Own in this Sacrament of Thy Love;
Have mercy upon us.

Be merciful,
Spare us, O LORD.

Be merciful,
Hear us, O LORD.

FOR so many unworthy Communions;
We offer our lamentations, O LORD.

For the great irreverence of Christians;
We offer our lamentations, O LORD.

For the continual blasphemies of the wicked;
We offer our lamentations, O LORD.

For the carelessness and neglect of Priests and people;
We offer our lamentations, O LORD.

For the unbelief of those who discern Thee not;
We offer our lamentations, O LORD.

WE sinners do beseech Thee to hear us, O LORD GOD, and that Thou wouldest have mercy upon us, and spare us;
We beseech Thee to hear us, Good LORD.

THAT Thou wouldest vouchsafe to accept this our act of sorrow and humility;
We beseech Thee to hear us, Good LORD.

That Thou wouldest increase faith and reverence in all people;
We beseech Thee to hear us, Good LORD.

That Thou wouldest endue all with ardent zeal for Thine honour and glory;
We beseech Thee to hear us, Good LORD.

That Thou wouldest incline the hearts of all to worship and receive Thee worthily;
We beseech Thee to hear us, Good LORD.

That Thou wouldest make known to all Thy love in this Holy Sacrament;
We beseech Thee to hear us, Good LORD.

O LAMB of GOD, That takest away the sins of the world;
Spare us, O LORD.

O LAMB of GOD, That takest away the sins of the world;
Graciously hear us, O LORD.

O LAMB of GOD, That takest away the sins of the world;
Have mercy upon us.

O CHRIST, hear us.
O CHRIST, *graciously hear us.*

LORD, have mercy upon us.
Christ, *have mercy upon us.*
Lord, have mercy upon us.

OUR Father, Which art in heaven, Hallowed be Thy Name. Thy kingdom come. Thy will be done in earth, as it is in Heaven. Give us this day our daily bread. And forgive us our trespasses, As we forgive them that trespass against us. And lead us not into temptation; But deliver us from evil. Amen.

O LORD, hear our prayer:
R̂. *And let our cry come unto Thee.*
℣. The Lord be with you:
R̂. *And with thy spirit.*

Let us pray.

O LORD Jesus Christ, Who, as Thou didst endure for our salvation the outrages of those who crucified Thee, so now endurest the irreverences of those who " discern Thee not," rather than withhold Thy Sacred Presence from our Altars ; grant us Thy grâce to bewail, with true sorrow of heart, the indignities committed against Thee ; and to repair, as far as lies in our power, and with devout love, the many dishonours Thou still continuest to receive in this adorable Mystery, Who livest and reignest, with the Father and the Holy Spirit, One God, world without end. *Amen.*

WE beseech Thee, O LORD, to have compassion upon us, and to inflame all our hearts with ardent love and zeal for Thine honour and glory; make us, through Thy grace, always so to believe and understand, to feel and firmly hold, to speak and think of the exceeding Mystery of this Blessed Sacrament, as shall be well pleasing to Thee, and profitable to our souls; may Thy Priests continually offer up this Holy Sacrifice in the beauty of holiness, and Thy people more and more with devotion and delight throng Thine Altars; and grant unto us all, that, worthily adoring and receiving Thee upon earth, we may finally, by Thy mercy, be admitted to the Heavenly Banquet, where Thou, "the LAMB Which is in the midst of the Throne," in unveiled Majesty, art perfectly worshipped and glorified by countless Angels and Saints, for ever and ever. *Amen.*

THE LORD be with you :

℟. *And with thy spirit.*

℣. May the Almighty and Merciful LORD graciously hear us.

℟. *Amen.*

℣. And may the souls of the Faithful Departed, through the Mercy of GOD, rest in peace.

℟. *Amen.*

Office for Spiritual Communion.

"But if a man, either by reason of extremity of sickness, or for want of warning in due time to the Curate, or for lack of company to receive with him, or by any other just impediment, do not receive the Sacrament of CHRIST'S Body and Blood, the Curate shall instruct him, that if he do truly repent him of his sins, and steadfastly believe that JESUS CHRIST hath suffered death upon the Cross for him, and shed His Blood for his redemption, earnestly remembering the benefits he hath thereby, and giving Him hearty thanks therefore, he doth eat and drink the Body and Blood of our SAVIOUR CHRIST profitably to his soul's health, although he do not receive the Sacrament with his mouth."—*Office of the Communion of the Sick in the Book of Common Prayer.*

It is suggested that the Act of Spiritual Communion be made, if possible, at the very time when it is known that the Eucharistic Sacrifice is being offered in some Church.

IN ✠ the Name of the FATHER, and of the SON, and of the HOLY GHOST. Amen.

OUR FATHER, Which art in Heaven, Hallowed be Thy Name. Thy kingdom come. Thy will be done in earth, as it is in Heaven. Give us this day our daily bread. And forgive us our trespasses, As we forgive them that trespass against us. And lead us not into temptation; But deliver us from evil. Amen.

I BELIEVE in GOD the FATHER Almighty, Maker of heaven and earth: And in JESUS CHRIST His only SON our LORD, Who was conceived by the HOLY GHOST, Born of the Virgin Mary, Suffered under Pontius Pilate, Was crucified, dead, and buried, He descended into hell; The third day He rose again from the dead, He ascended into heaven, And sitteth on the right hand of GOD the FATHER Almighty; from thence He shall come to judge the quick and the dead.

I believe in the HOLY GHOST; The holy Catholic Church; The Communion of Saints; The Forgiveness of sins; The Resurrection of the body; And the life everlasting. Amen.

O GOD, make speed to save us:
R̷. O LORD, *make haste to help us.*

Glory be to the FATHER, and to the SON, and to the HOLY GHOST;

As it was in the beginning, is now, and ever shall be : world without end. Amen.
Alleluia.

Or, from Septuagesima to Easter ;

Praise be to Thee, O LORD, King of eternal glory.

One or more of the Psalms following may then be used.

Antiphon. To him that overcometh.

PSALM XXIII.   *Dominus regit me.*

THE LORD is my Shepherd : therefore can I lack nothing.

He shall feed me in a green pasture : and lead me forth beside the waters of comfort.

He shall convert my soul : and bring me forth in the paths of righteousness, for His Name's sake.

Yea, though I walk through the valley of the shadow of death, I will fear no evil : for Thou art with me : Thy rod and Thy staff comfort me.

Thou shalt prepare a Table before me against them that trouble me : Thou hast anointed my head with oil, and my cup shall be full.

But Thy loving-kindness and mercy shall follow me all the days of my life : and I will dwell in the house of the LORD for ever.

Glory be to the FATHER, and to the SON : and to the HOLY GHOST;

As it was in the beginning, is now, and ever shall be : world without end. Amen.

Or, PSALM XLII.   *Quemadmodum.*

LIKE as the hart desireth the water-brooks : so longeth my soul after Thee, O GOD.

My soul is athirst for GOD, yea, even for the living GOD : when shall I come to appear before the presence of GOD?

My tears have been my meat day and night : while they daily say unto me, Where is now thy GOD?

Now when I think thereupon, I pour out my heart by myself : for I went with the multitude, and brought them forth into the house of GOD;

In the voice of praise and thanksgiving : among such as keep holy-day.

Why art thou so full of heaviness, O my soul : and why art thou so disquieted within me?

Put thy trust in GOD : for I will yet give Him thanks for the help of His countenance.

My GOD, my soul is vexed within me : therefore will I remember Thee concerning the land of Jordan, and the little hill of Hermon.

One deep calleth another, because of the

noise of the water-pipes : all Thy waves and storms are gone over me.

The LORD hath granted His loving-kindness in the day-time : and in the night-season did I sing of Him, and made my prayer unto the GOD of my life.

I will say unto the GOD of my strength, Why hast Thou forgotten me : why go I thus heavily, while the enemy oppresseth me?

My bones are smitten asunder as with a sword : while mine enemies that trouble me cast me in the teeth;

Namely, while they say daily unto me : Where is now thy GOD?

Why art thou so vexed, O my soul : and why art thou so disquieted within me?

O put thy trust in GOD : for I will yet thank Him, which is the help of my countenance, and my GOD.

Glory be to the FATHER, and to the SON : and to the HOLY GHOST;

As it was in the beginning, is now, and ever shall be : world without end. Amen.

Or, Psalm cxi., *Confitebor Tibi*, *p.* 20, *and* Psalm xliii., *Judica me, Deus, p.* 24.

Antiphon. To him that overcometh will I give to eat of the Tree of Life, which is in the midst of the Paradise of GOD. *During Easter*, Alleluia.

SHORT LESSON. *S. John* vi. 53.

THEN JESUS said unto them, Verily, verily, I say unto you, Except ye eat the Flesh of the SON of Man, and drink His Blood, ye have no life in you.

Whoso eateth My flesh, and drinketh My Blood, hath eternal life, and I will raise him up at the last day.

For My Flesh is meat indeed, and My Blood is drink indeed. He that eateth My Flesh and drinketh My Blood, dwelleth in Me, and I in him.

Ry. *Thanks be to* GOD.

Responsory. Elijah looked, and, behold, there was a cake baken on the coals, and a cruse of water at his head; and he arose, and did eat and drink. And he went in the strength of that meat forty days and forty nights, unto Horeb the mount of GOD. [Alleluia.]

Ƴ. If any man eat of this Bread, he shall live for ever.

Ry. *And he went in the strength of that meat forty days and forty nights, unto Horeb the Mount of* GOD.

Ƴ. Glory be to the FATHER, and to the SON : and to the HOLY GHOST.

Ry. *Unto Horeb the mount of* GOD. [*Alleluia.*]

HYMN.   *Verbum Supernum prodiens.*

The Heavenly Word proceeding forth,
 Yet leaving not the FATHER'S side,
Accomplishing His work on earth,
 Had reached at length life's eventide.

By false disciple to be given
 To foemen for His life athirst;
Himself the very Bread of Heaven,
 He gave to His disciples first.

He gave Himself in either Kind,
 His precious Flesh, His precious Blood,
In love's own fulness thus designed
 Of the whole man to be the Food.

By birth their fellow-man was He,
 Their Meat when sitting at the board;
He died their Ransomer to be,
 He ever reigns, their great Reward.

O saving Victim, opening wide
 The gate of Heaven to man below;
Our foes press on from every side,
 Thine aid supply, Thy strength bestow.

Blest Three in One, to Thee ascend
 All thanks and praise for evermore;
Oh, grant us life that shall not end
 Upon the Heavenly Country's shore.
       Amen.

Or any other Eucharistic Hymn.

℣. The LORD hath done great things for
 us.   [Alleluia.]

R℣. *Whereof we rejoice.* [*Alleluia.*]

Antiphon. JESUS said, Come unto Me.

MAGNIFICAT. *S. Luke* i.

MY soul doth magnify the LORD : and my spirit hath rejoiced in GOD my SAVIOUR.

For He hath regarded : the lowliness of His handmaiden.

For behold, from henceforth : all generations shall call me blessed.

For He that is mighty hath magnified me : and holy is His Name.

And His mercy is on them that fear Him : throughout all generations.

He hath showed strength with His arm : He hath scattered the proud in the imagination of their hearts.

He hath put down the mighty from their seat : and hath exalted the humble and meek.

He hath filled the hungry with good things : and the rich He hath sent empty away.

He remembering His mercy hath holpen His servant Israel : as He promised to our forefathers, Abraham and his seed, for ever.

Glory be to the FATHER, and to the SON : and to the HOLY GHOST ;

As it was in the beginning, is now, and ever shall be : world without end. Amen.

Antiphon. JESUS said, Come unto Me, all that travail, and are heavy laden, and I will refresh you.   Alleluia.

LORD, have mercy upon us.
CHRIST, *have mercy upon us.*
LORD, have mercy upon us.

OUR FATHER, Which art in Heaven, Hallowed be Thy Name. Thy kingdom come. Thy will be done in earth, as it is in Heaven. Give us this day our daily bread. And forgive us our trespasses, As we forgive them that trespass against us. And lead us not into temptation; But deliver us from evil.   Amen.

O LAMB of GOD, That takest away the sins of the world;
Have mercy upon us.
O LAMB of GOD, That takest away the sins of the world;
Have mercy upon us.
O LAMB of GOD, That takest away the sins of the world;
Grant us Thy peace.

O LORD JESU CHRIST, SON of the Living GOD, interpose Thy Passion, Cross, and Death between Thy judgment and my soul, now, and in the hour of my death. Vouchsafe to give me grace and mercy; pardon to the living; rest to the dead; peace and concord to Thy Church; and to all sinners, life and glory everlasting; Who livest and reignest with GOD the FATHER in the Unity of the HOLY SPIRIT, one GOD, world without end. *Amen.*

Here meditate devoutly on the Passion and Death of JESUS CHRIST; or on the Real Presence of His Sacred Body and Blood in the Holy Eucharist, or on the Holy Sacrifice of Himself therein continually offered before the FATHER.

Then lift up your heart unto the LORD, using such ejaculations and aspirations as the following:

O LORD JESU CHRIST, what great things hast Thou done, what hast Thou endured, from the force of Thy boundless love towards me! But what return have I made? or what shall I make unto Thee?

I mourn from my inmost heart that I ever sinned against Thee, Who hast so greatly loved me.

I believe in Thee with lively faith, O Thou eternal Truth! that Thou Thyself art GOD and MAN, my LORD, and my SAVIOUR!

I hope in Thee, O LORD, O Thou the only hope and true Salvation of my soul!

I will love Thee, O LORD my Strength, above all things, with my whole heart, O Thou Lover of my soul!

Whom have I in heaven but Thee? and there is none upon earth that I desire in comparison of Thee!

Like as the hart desireth the water-brooks, so longeth my soul after Thee, O GOD.

What is man, that Thou art mindful of him; or the son of man, that Thou visitest him?

Blessed is He that cometh in the **Name** of the LORD.

Then say:

LORD, I am not worthy that Thou shouldest enter under my roof; but speak the word only, and Thy servant shall be healed.

Acts of Spiritual Communion.

O MOST loving JESU, I believe that Thou art truly present in the most Holy Sacrament of the Altar. I adore Thee; I love Thee. Since I cannot now be present at the Holy Eucharist, and receive Thee sacramentally, I most earnestly desire to partake of Thee spiritually. Come to my poor soul. Unite Thyself to me . . . ✠ . . . O my JESU, my soul rejoices in Thee; my soul blesses Thee. O never leave me. Amen.

Or,

IN union, O Dear Lord, with the faithful at every Altar of Thy Church, where Thy Blessed Body and Blood are being offered to the Father, I desire to offer Thee praise and thanksgiving. I present to Thee my soul and body, with the earnest wish that I may be always united to Thee. And since I cannot now receive Thee sacramentally, I beseech Thee to come spiritually into my heart. I unite myself to Thee, and embrace Thee with all the affections of my soul. O let nothing ever separate Thee from me. Let me live and die in Thy love. Amen.

Then add:

Rhythm. Anima Christi.

SOUL of Christ, sanctify me :
　Body of Christ, save me :
Blood of Christ, inebriate me :
Water from the Side of Christ, wash me :
Passion of Christ, strengthen me :
O Good Jesu, hear me :
Within Thy Wounds hide me :
Suffer me not to be separated from Thee :
From the malicious enemy defend me :
In the hour of my death call me,
And bid me come to Thee :
That with Thy Saints I may praise Thee
For all eternity. Amen.

Further Ejaculations and Aspirations.

ABIDE with me, O my Lord and my All!
On Thee alone may my heart be fixed;
in Thee be my rest; O forsake me not.

Let my soul, O Lord, be ever filled with
the sweetness of Thy Presence; and con-
strained by love of Thee, seek for nought
wherein to joy, out of Thee, O Thou true
Felicity.

O Sweet Jesu, very God, very Man, in
Thee and with Thee I can do all things!
Thou dwellest in me, of whom then shall
I be afraid? Thy grace is sufficient for
me; in Thy strength then will I go forth.

O Lord, let Thy mercy be showed upon
me; as I do put my trust in Thee.

A Prayer for Various Graces.

O MIGHTY God, O God All-powerful,
All-gracious, Whom all must believe
and know Unchangeable, Incorruptible; O
Trinity in Unity, by the Catholic Church
worshipped and adored, I dedicate myself
unto Thee; O make me Thine, and keep
me Thine for ever. Grant me, Gracious
Lord, a pure intention of my heart, and a
single eye to Thy glory, in all my actions;
possess my soul with Thy presence, and
ravish it with Thy Love.

Be Thou a Light unto mine eyes, and
Music to mine ears: Sweetness to my taste,

and a full Contentment to my heart. Be
Thou my Sunshine in the daytime, my Re-
pose at night, a Shadow in the heat, and a
Shelter from the cold, my Food in hunger,
my Clothing in nakedness, and a Refuge
in every time of trouble.

O Lord God, I give unto Thee my body,
soul, and spirit, to be Thine for ever, in
sickness and in health, in poverty and
wealth, in fulness and in want, in life and
in death. I give Thee my substance and
my friends, and all that I have. Use me
for Thyself, and for the glory of Thy
blessed Name. Dispose of me, as seemeth
good unto Thee ; I am not mine own, but
Thine, therefore claim me as Thy right,
keep me as Thy charge, and love me as
Thy child. Fight for me when I am as-
saulted, heal me when I am wounded, re-
vive me when I am destroyed.

My Lord and my God ! I beseech Thee
to give me patience in adversities, humility
in comforts, constancy in temptations, and
victory over all my ghostly enemies. Grant
me sorrow for my sins, thankfulness for
Thy benefits, fear of Thy judgments, love
of Thy mercies, and mindfulness of Thy
presence evermore. Make me humble to
my superiors, and friendly to my equals,
charitable to my enemies, and loving to
my friends, ready to please all, and loath
to offend any.

Give me modesty in my countenance, gravity in my behaviour, deliberation in my speech, holiness in my thoughts, and righteousness in all my actions; let Thy mercy cleanse me from my sins, and Thy grace produce in me the fruits of everlasting life.

Give me, O LORD, an obedient spirit, and a teachable mind; let me be cheerful without lightness, sorrowful yet rejoicing, fearing Thee without doubting, and trusting Thee without presumption. Let me be joyful at nothing but that which pleaseth Thee, and sorrowful for nothing but that which doth displease Thee; let labour for Thee be my delight, and all rest be a weariness out of Thee. Give me a waking spirit, and a diligent soul, that I may seek to know Thy will, and when I know it, may perform it faithfully, to the honour and glory of Thy ever-blessed Name. Amen.

For the Church.

O GOD, Who wonderfully refreshest Thy Church by Thy Precious Body and Blood; pour out upon it Thy Quickening SPIRIT, that, living upon Thee on earth through partaking of the Heavenly Mysteries, we may attain to live with Thee in Heaven, Who livest and reignest with the FATHER and the HOLY GHOST, One GOD, world without end. Amen.

*Here Special Intercessions and other prayers
may be added.*

LET us bless the LORD.
℞. *Thanks be to* GOD.

MAY the souls of the Faithful Departed,
through the Mercy of GOD, rest in
peace.
℞. *Amen.*

Short Office for Spiritual Communion.

IN ✠ the Name of the FATHER, and of
the SON, and of the HOLY GHOST.
Amen.

OUR FATHER, Which art in Heaven, Hallowed be Thy Name. Thy kingdom
come. Thy will be done in earth, as it is
in Heaven. Give us this day our daily
bread. And forgive us our trespasses, As
we forgive them that trespass against us.
And lead us not into temptation; But deliver us from evil. Amen.

I BELIEVE in GOD the FATHER Almighty, Maker of Heaven and earth:
And in JESUS CHRIST His only SON our
LORD, Who was conceived by the HOLY
GHOST, Born of the Virgin Mary, Suffered
under Pontius Pilate, Was crucified, dead,
and buried, He descended into Hell; The
third day He rose again from the dead,
He ascended into Heaven, And sitteth on
the right hand of GOD the FATHER Almighty; from thence He shall come to
judge the quick and the dead.
I believe in the HOLY GHOST; The holy
Catholic Church; the Communion of

Saints; The Forgiveness of sins; The Resurrection of the body; And the life everlasting. Amen.

Antiphon. To him that overcometh. Ps. xxiii., The LORD is my Shepherd, &c., *p.* 64.

O LORD JESU CHRIST, I mourn from my inmost heart that I ever sinned against Thee, and resolve by Thy grace to forsake sin.

BLESSED be Thou, O. LORD JESU CHRIST, SON of the Living GOD, Who, in Thy pity for us, didst come down from heaven, and on the Altar of the Cross didst freely offer Thy Body and Blood, Which Thou hadst taken of the Virgin, as a true Sacrifice for our sins.

PRAISE and glory be to Thee, because of the Same Thy Body and Blood which Thou hast ordained not only that we should partake as the Bread of Life in the Sacrament, but that a Sacrifice should be offered upon the Altar by Thy Priests, and be celebrated even unto the end of the world.

Here meditate on the Holy Sacrifice offered on the Altars of the Church; or on the Communion of our LORD there really Present and given to us, or on His promise, " If any man love Me, he will keep My words, and My FATHER will love him, and We will come unto him, and make Our abode with him."

Then say:

LORD, I am not worthy that Thou shouldest enter under my roof; but speak the word only, and Thy servant shall be healed.

Act of Spiritual Communion.

IN union, O Dear LORD, with the faithful at every Altar of Thy Church, where Thy Blessed Body and Blood are being offered to the FATHER, I desire to offer Thee praise and thanksgiving. I present to Thee my soul and body with the earnest wish that I may be always united to Thee. And since I cannot now receive Thee sacramentally, I beseech Thee to come spiritually into my heart. I unite myself to Thee, and embrace Thee with all the affections of my soul. O let nothing ever separate Thee from me. Let me live and die in Thy Love. Amen.

Then add:

BLESS ye the LORD, all ye works of His; bless the LORD, O my soul, and all that is within me, bless His holy Name. O that I might love Thee, and give thanks unto Thee, and my whole spirit might praise Thee, O LORD, with the fervour of all Angels and Saints.

A Prayer for Grace.

O MERCIFUL LORD GOD, Who dost vouchsafe to feed us, Thy unworthy creatures, with that Bread which cometh down from Heaven, and giveth life unto the soul; so strengthen and sustain me, I beseech Thee, by Thy most gracious gifts, that I may resist all the temptations of the world, the flesh, and the devil, and walking in the way of Thy commandments, may glorify Thy Holy Name; through JESUS CHRIST our LORD. Amen.

The Blessing.

THE Grace of our LORD JESUS CHRIST, and the Love of GOD, and the Fellowship of the HOLY GHOST, be with us all evermore.

R̲. *Amen.*

J. MASTERS and SON, Printers,
Albion Buildings, Bartholomew Close, London, E.C.

www.ingramcontent.com/pod-product-compliance
Lightning Source LLC
Chambersburg PA
CBHW020327090426
42735CB00009B/1437